Garfield gains weight

BY: JIM DAVIS

BALLANTINE BOOKS · NEW YORK

P9-DMT-585

COPYRIGHT© 1981 BY UNITED FEATURES SYNDICATE, INC.

ALL RIGHTS RESERVED UNDER INTERNATIONAL AND PAN-AMERICAN COPYRIGHT
CONVENTIONS. PUBLISHED IN THE UNITED STATES BY BALLANTINE BOOKS,
A DIVISION OF RANDOM HOUSE, INC., NEW YORK, AND SIMULTANEOUSLY IN CANADA
BY RANDOM HOUSE OF CANADA, LIMITED, TORONTO, CANADA.

LIBRARY OF CONGRESS CATALOG CARD NUMBER: 80-69730

ISBN 0-345-28844-0

MANUFACTURED IN THE UNITED STATES OF AMERICA

FIRST BALLANTINE BOOKS EDITION MARCH 1981

8 9

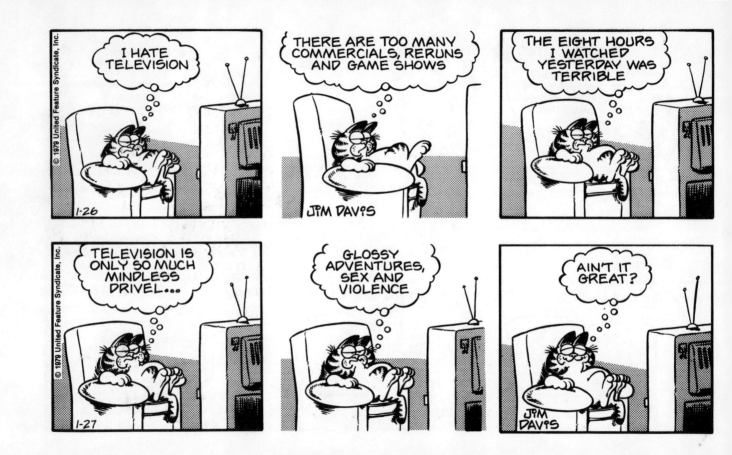

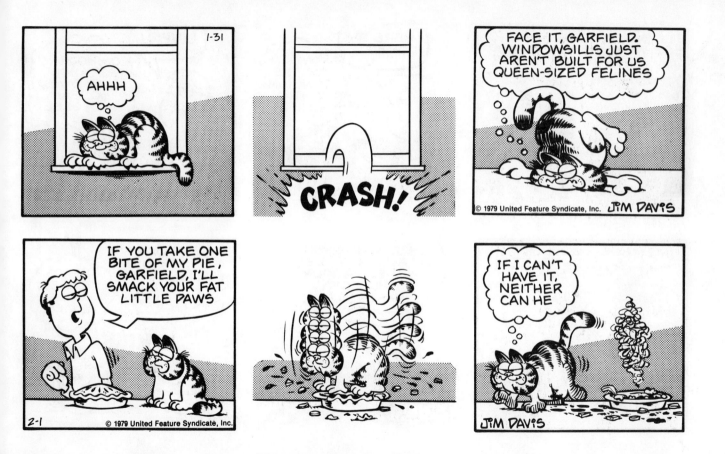

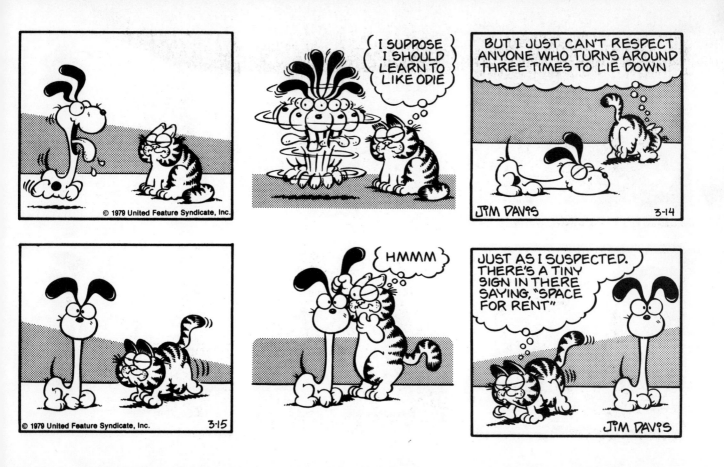

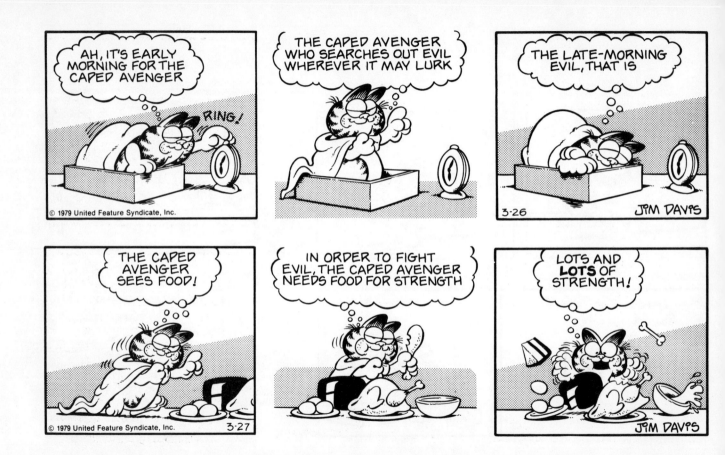

© 1979 United Feature Syndicate, Inc.

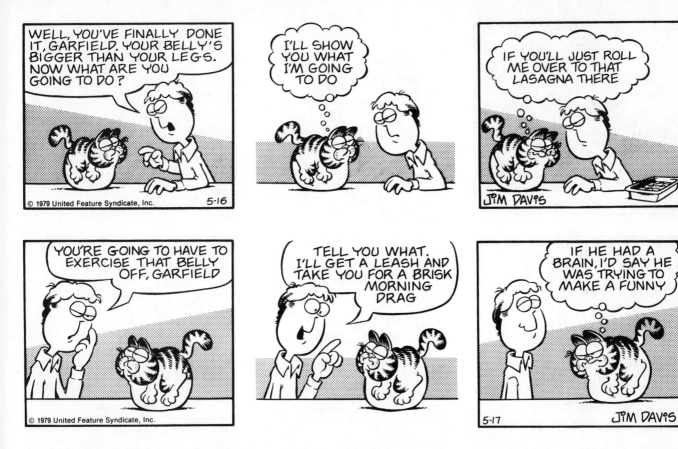

© 1979 United Feature Syndicate, Inc. 5-18

BOING BOING B...

JIM DAVIS

AT LAST! MY FEET CAN TOUCH THE FLOOR ONCE MORE

JIM DAVIS 5-19

NEVER AGAIN WILL I ALLOW MYSELF TO GET THAT FAT

© 1979 United Feature Syndicate, Inc.

AND IF YOU BELIEVE THAT, I HAVE A BRIDGE TO SELL YOU

DID I EVER TELL YOU ABOUT MY UNCLE HARRY? HE WAS A FAMOUS MOUSER AT A GLASS PLANT IN GAS CITY, INDIANA

5-23 © 1979 United Feature Syndicate, Inc.

LEGEND HAS IT THAT UNCLE HARRY CHASED A MOUSE RIGHT INTO TANK #2

NOW HE'S A PAPERWEIGHT IN BAYONNE, NEW JERSEY

JIM DAVIS

GRAB!

JIM DAVIS

BONK!

© 1979 United Feature Syndicate, Inc.

SMOOTH MOVE OL' BUDDY

HAVE YOU NO RESPECT FOR THE DEAD?

5-24

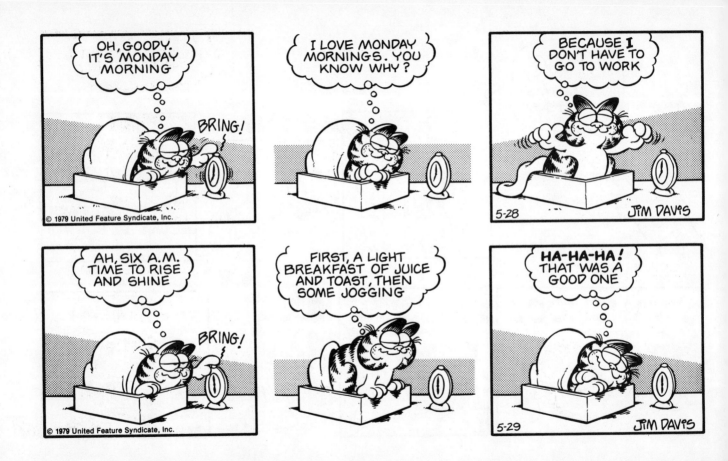

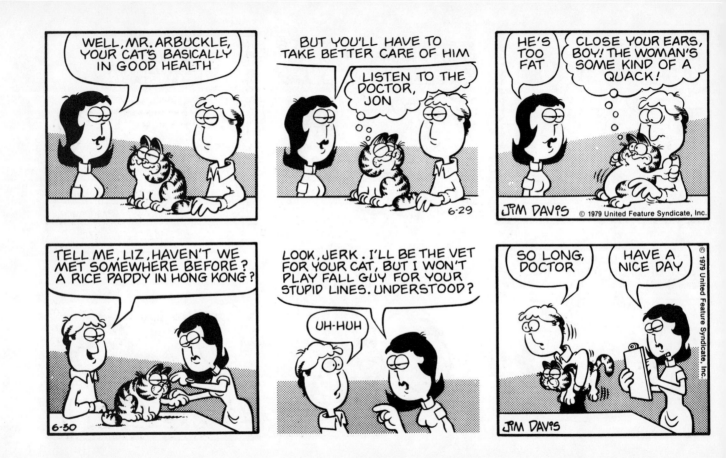

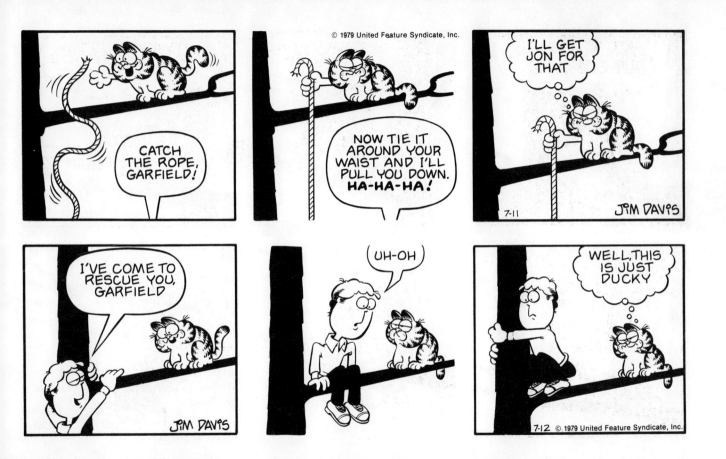

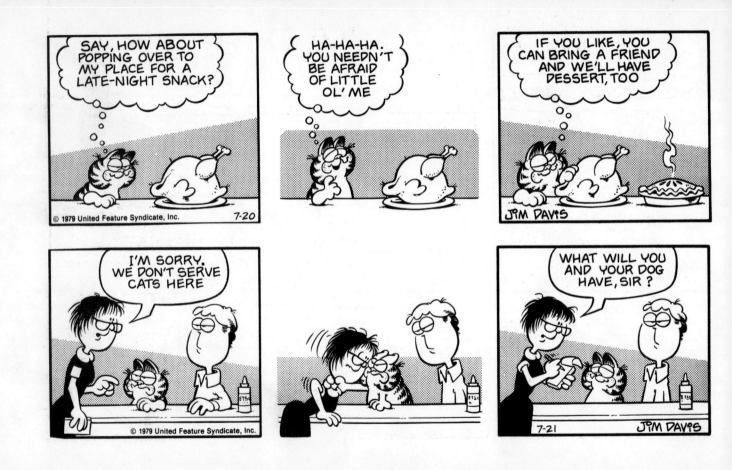

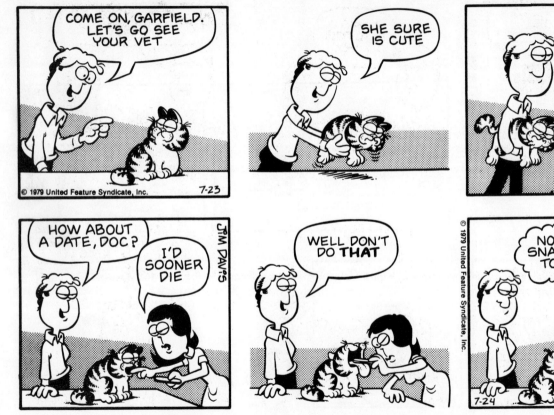

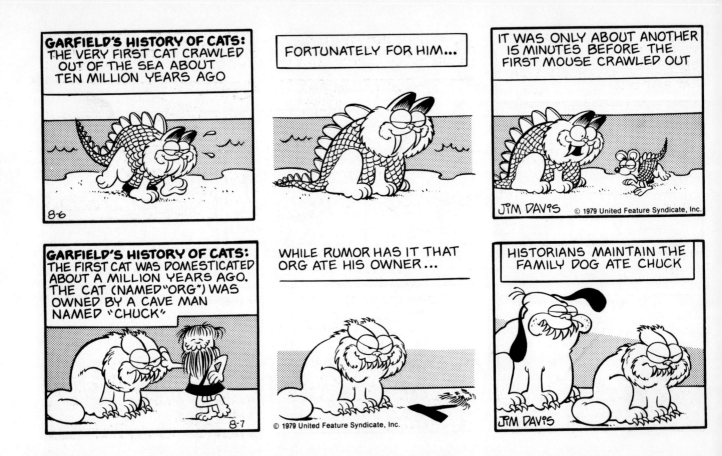

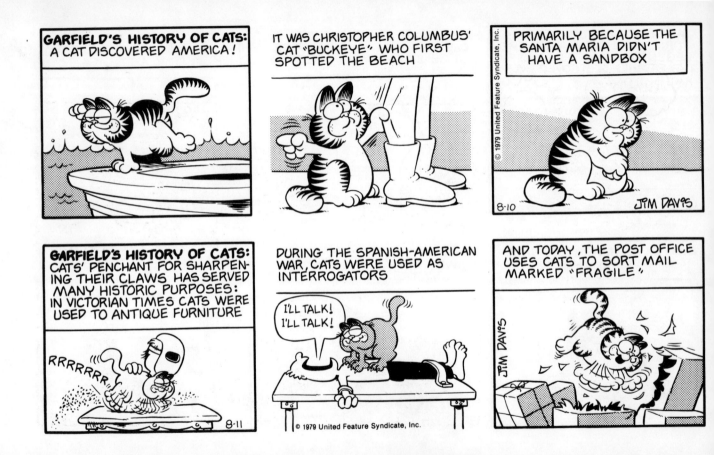

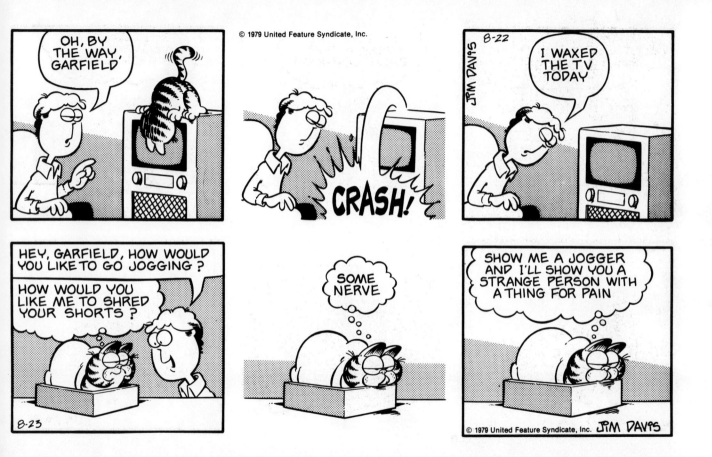

A Talk with Jim Davis:
Most Asked Questions

How far in advance do you do the strip?

"Eight to ten weeks—no less, no more. I operate on what Al Capp termed 'the ragged edge of disaster.'"

When did GARFIELD first appear in newspapers?

"June 19, 1978."

Do you own a cat? A GARFIELD?

"No. My wife, Carolyn, is allergic to cats. However, I did grow up on a farm with about 25 cats."

Where do you get your ideas for the strip?

"I glean a lot of good ideas from fan mail. Cat owners are very proud of their cats and supply a generous amount of cat stories."

What GARFIELD products are on the market and in production?

"Books, calendars, T-shirts, coffee mugs, posters, tote bags, greeting cards, puzzles…in another few months GARFIELD will be on everything but pantyhose and TVs."

Why a cat?

"Aside from the obvious reasons, that I know and love cats, I noticed there were a lot of comic-strip dogs who were commanding their share of the comic pages but precious few cats. It seemed like a good idea."

Where did you get the name GARFIELD?

"My grandfather's name was James A. Garfield Davis. The name GARFIELD to me sounds like a fat cat…or a St. Bernard…or a neat line of thermal underwear."

What did you do for a living before GARFIELD?

"I was assistant on the comic strip TUMBLEWEEDS and a free-lance commercial artist."

What's your sign?

"Leo, of course, the sign of the cat."

Have you ever been convicted of a felony?

"Next question, please."

Are you subject to fainting spells, seizures, and palpitations?

"Only when I work."

Have you ever spent time in a mental institution?

"Yes, I visit my comics editor there."

Do you advocate the overthrow of our government by violent means?

"No, but I have given consideration to vandalizing my local license branch."

Are you hard of hearing?

"Huh?"

Do you wish to donate an organ?

"Heck no, but I have a piano I can let go cheap."